Contents

Acknowledgments

Images and photographs have been reproduced with the kind permission of: Philip Clarke, Heather James, Rebecca Lewis, Nona Rees, Jerry Sampson and Joan Tate.
Published by Red Dot Design Publications in October 2012
Design: Red Dot Design
Print: Harcourt Colour Print
ISBN: 978-0-9573842-1-7 ©St Davids Cathedral

INTRODUCTION
by the Very Revd Jonathan Lean, Dean of St Davids

It can be easy for a modern tourist to forget that this extraordinary place is not merely a series of historic buildings in a beautiful landscape. St Davids is, above all, a living church and a centre of faith that has attracted millions of people for almost 1,500 years. Everything you see here is a visible expression of the worship of God. Over the centuries, it has been a retreat from the outside world, a centre of power and wealth and the scene of turmoil and decay. Today, the Cathedral lies at the heart of a vibrant community encompassing the city that bears its name, the nation whose patron saint lived and died here. Here visitors and pilgrims have found peace and a new sense of purpose in this place of prayer and contemplation.

St David's simplicity of living, his devotion to prayer and worship, has resonated with the minds and souls of Christians of every generation. Those final words which he spoke on his deathbed: 'Be joyful, keep the faith and do the little things' speak to us today, as much as they did to those who gathered around him at his last hour. David's life and legacy to the Church and to the nation is something to be valued and celebrated.

David's life, his legacy to the people of God and his faithful witness to the message of the Gospel was made an example for all through the building of a shrine to his name. Pope Calixtus II transformed this place by his declaration that two pilgrimages to St Davids were equivalent to one to Rome, three to St Davids equivalent to one to Jerusalem. Here for centuries pilgrims came in their thousands and thousands to offer prayer and praise to God. Here pilgrims came to ask for healing, for strength, for the ability to carry on with their sometimes difficult lives. The destruction of the shrine removed so much of that wonderful ministry, of that opportunity for people to encounter God in their lives, but the pilgrims continued to come, albeit in small numbers.

It was for these reasons that I wanted to restore the Shrine of St David. To offer to the hundreds of thousands of people who visit this place an opportunity to learn about St David, about his message to the people of Wales and about his faith in God who is our creator and redeemer. I wished to place pilgrimage back at the heart of our ministry here, so that through worship, prayer and thanksgiving we might build up the body of Christ.

So many thousands of people visit St Davids Cathedral and enjoy the beauty of the building and its surroundings, but I want them to do more than that. Through the restoration of the Shrine I hope that the Church in this place will be able to transform those visitors into pilgrims.

THE HISTORY OF THE SHRINE
by Jerry Sampson, Cathedral Archaeologist

Geraldus Cambrensis said of the Welsh in his *'Descriptio Cambrensis'*,

'...they pay greater respect than any other people to their churches, to men in orders, the relics of saints, bishops' crooks, bells, holy books and the Cross itself.'

- an account which stresses not only the importance of the sort of relics which we might normally think of in the context of medieval shrines - the actual physical remains, the bones and bodies of the saints - but also of their non-corporal relics, the possessions and symbols of authority which these holy men and women once owned.

Even in the aftermath of the Norman Conquest of Wales the Welsh maintained their respect for the churches and priests, even in regard to the recently 'planted' monasteries founded by their Norman overlords. Gilbert Foliot, abbot of Gloucester (1139-48) wrote to Osbern, who may have been Prior of Ewenny, *'the best specimen of a fortified ecclesiastical building...'* [1]

"I recommend you to strengthen the locks of your doors and surround your house with a good ditch and an impregnable wall lest that people which as you say, gazes with shaggy brow and fierce eyes, break into it and destroy with one blow all your labour and sweat... We see, indeed, our own people take little account of the fear of God and reverence for his sanctuary but we hear that they [the Welsh] diligently honour holy places and persons consecrated to God. Because of all these things it is hard for us to be planted by those who hardly care, only to be rooted out by those who honour us." [2]

Canon Bazely says that following the Norman Conquest,

"The Welsh seem to have treated the monasteries and churches of Glamorgan with respect, and whilst they lost no opportunity of destroying the castle of an alien lord, and were always more or less in a state of feud amongst themselves, they gave but little annoyance to the secular and religious clergy. Margam, Neath and Ewenny were almost always at their mercy, if they had chosen to destroy them, but we only hear now and then of a raid on a barton (monastic farm) and the theft of a few cattle." [3]

---

1   Professor E.A. Freeman, "Architectural Antiquities in Glamorganshire - No.2: Coyty, Coychurch, and Ewenny", in Archaeologia Cambrensis, vol.3, 3rd series (1857), p.114.

2   Letter from Gilbert Foliot to Prior Osbern, quoted in F.G.Cowey, 'The Church from the Norman Conquest to the Beginning of the 14th-century', in T.B. Pugh (ed), 'Glamorgan County History: III, The Middle Ages', Cardiff 1971, pp.87-135.

3   Rev. Canon Bazeley, "Early Connection Between Glamorgan and Gloucestershire", Transactions of the Bristol and Gloucestershire Archaeological Society, 1908, p.49.

This habit of respect for churches and the persons of clerics had a long pedigree, and pervades also the attitude of the Celtic church to its shrines, so that for the Celtic church the bodies and physical remains of the saints were not generally the central objects of reverence or pilgrimage. As Heather James points out:

'...to the Welsh as well as the Bretons, physical relics of the saints were not essential to their cults but that 'features of the landscape and bells and crosses were the focal points for saints' cults, not bones and shrines...' [4]

Thus it was that,

'Generally speaking, the early church in Wales buried its saints, preserving and revering objects associated with them during their lifetimes such as bells, books, staffs and clothing. The Norman church brought a change of emphasis, venerating the physical remains of saints and elevating their status as relics.' [5]

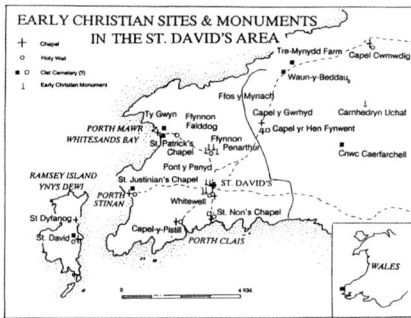

EARLY CHRISTIAN SITES & MONUMENTS IN THE ST. DAVID'S AREA

The ancient Christian ritual landscape of St Davids, as reconstructed by Heather James, with the sea-girt *temenos* of St Davids Head bounded to the east by the Ffos y Mynach and centred on the Cathedral site, contains a wealth of chapels, holy wells, cist cemeteries and early Christian monuments. Glastonbury, also an early monastic complex bounded to the west by marsh-lands liable to flood, and, like Dyfed, also perhaps with Irish connections in the early middle ages, presents a parallel arrangement, with a group of satellite chapels and the ditch of Ponter's Ball defining the perimeter of the sacred enclosure to the east.

St Davids must have been an important centre of pilgrimage and learning from very early times; indeed, when Alfred the Great sought to reinvigorate Christianity in Wessex it was to Asser at St Davids that he turned in the late ninth century.

In such a context, pilgrimage and the display of relics must have been an important aspect of St Davids from earliest times. Relics were certainly being venerated at the Cathedral in the eleventh century, since in 1081 Gruffuth ap Cynan and Rhys ap Teudur *'went together to the church of David to pray. There they became faithful friends, after swearing on the relics...'* [6]

---

4   Heather James, 'The Cult of St David in the Middle Ages', quoting Smith 1990.

5   Terry John and Nona Rees, 'Pilgrimage: A Welsh Perspective'.

6   History of Gruff. ap Cynan, pp.124-30 in Acts p.234, D.7.

The first certain reference to a shrine at the Cathedral occurs in 1088, when a reliquary was stolen and despoiled of the gold and silver with which it was covered. It is difficult to be certain what this shrine looked like: there is a sketch by Edward Lluyd (c.1696) of a probable eighth century Welsh shrine casket from Gwytherin (now lost), and, from Ireland, the surviving twelfth century Shrine of St Manchan from Boher church, county Offaly. The latter has rings at the base to allow poles to be passed through for carrying the shrine-casket in processions, and we know that one of St David's shrines was also portable, since it was carried into battle.

Of the known relics associated with St David himself there is his bell, 'Bangu', which was once kept at Glascwm, Montgomeryshire, and his staff, once kept at Llanddewi Brefi. In a monastic world where the day was ordered by the ringing of bells, and at a time in the sixth century when bell-towers probably did not exist, the hand-bell was an obvious indication of a bishop's authority, and this and the pastoral staff were traditionally the outward signs of the Celtic bishop. An eighth or ninth century effigy of a bishop from White Island, Co. Fermanagh, depicts just such a bishop holding crozier and bell.

The third relic directly associated with St David is the enigmatic 'sapphire altar',

'This was a portable altar given to St David by the Patriarch of Jerusalem, '...being potent with miracles', and after the saint's death was kept hidden, 'concealed by coverings of skins' and 'never seen...by men'.

In the 1120s, William of Malmesbury wrote that the saint had bequeathed the altar to Glastonbury during his lifetime and that the case in which it had been kept remained in the diocese of Menevia. However, in the later *'Life of St David'* written at the end of the twelfth century by Giraldus Cambrensis, the altar was apparently in Llangyfelach. This Glastonbury altar was hidden in time of war and then rediscovered in a doorway of St Mary's church by Henry of Blois, (d.1171).He adorned it richly with silver and precious stones, though history does not record who gave the magnificent sapphire after which it was named.

'...on 25 May 1539 a 'superaltarre, garnished with silver and gilte, caled the great saphire of Glassonburye' was delivered to King Henry VIII.'[7]

If these three are the main objects associated with St David, what then of his corporeal relics?

In common with a huge number of other saints, Glastonbury claimed to possess the actual body of David. Glastonbury Abbey, 'the tomb of saints', regarded herself as the repository of a major collection of the corporeal relics of early saints, usually claiming that these had been brought to Somerset for safekeeping in time of war or in the aftermath of Viking raids. Thus it was, according to William of Malmesbury that in 962,

---

7   Terry John and Nona Rees, 2002.

'...a certain dame named Aelswitha, in the reign of King Edgar, acquired the said relics [of the body of St David] through a relative of hers, who at that time was bishop over Ross [Rhos] valley when all that district was so devastated that scarce one mortal could be found in it, only a few women, and these in few places, and she placed the relics at Glastonbury.' [8]

Bishop Bernard [bishop from 1115-48] had instigated searches for the body of St David during his episcopate - as William of Malmesbury says, *'Bishop Bernard sought his body many times, but despite the many claims could not find it'* [9] - and it remained to divine guidance in the later thirteenth century to provide the focus of devotion which generated the existing shrine-base.

'The inception of the present monument seems to have occurred in 1275 when John de Gamages, then prior of Ewenny, was instructed in a dream to dig at a certain place just outside the south door of the present cathedral church.... Following Prior John's vision a body was duly discovered and a feretrum prepared; it must have been complete by 1284 when Edward I and Queen Eleanor came to St Davids 'on pilgrimage'. It was presumably on that occasion that Edward acquired an arm of the saint.' [10]

The existing shrine is clearly designed for its present location, fitting centrally within the north choir arcade, with a southern 'show' elevation richly decorated with triple arcading facing into the ritual space of the presbytery, and a simpler north elevation facing into the aisle.

The shrine superficially resembles a group of shrine-bases with *foramina* - porthole-like openings in the side elevations. These openings enabled pilgrims to get as close as possible to the relics of the saint interred within or beneath the shrine. In a world of faith where medicine didn't really work, an important aspect of pilgrimage to a saint's shrine in the middle ages was that of seeking a cure for illness and affliction, and the closer the affected part of the body could come to the beneficent radiation of the relics, the more likely a miraculous cure might become. Several shrine-bases of this type survive, such as those at Salisbury Cathedral (St Osmund), Whitchurch Canonicorum in Dorset (St Wite), and Ilam in Staffordshire (St Bertelin); and medieval depictions of the early shrines of St Edward the Confessor (Westminster) and St Thomas Becket (Canterbury) are also of this form.

How did the monument function in the middle ages? John Crook has considered the practicalities which the design of the existing shrine-base addressed,

---

8   This corresponds to the period 961-999, during which, according to Jones and Freeman, 'St Davids was harassed by a continual series of assaults on the part of the Northmen, in one of which Bishop Morgeneu was slain.' [p.266].

9   William of Malmesbury, De Gestis Regum, vol.1, p.28 - in Acts p.267 (D143)

10   John Crook.

front of the shrine before its restoration

The rear of the shrine before its restoration

'It is scarcely necessary to emphasise that despite its superficial resemblance to a foramina shrine, the alleged relics of St David could never have been placed below or indeed within the body of the monument. In any case, references like the account of his bones being borne in battle suggest that they were in an easily moved ferretrum. The simplest solution is that the reliquary was small enough to be normally parked on top of the mensa in the central bay of the arcaded reredos, partly protected by the arcading above. This is a space only 600 mm wide by 660 deep, but there is no reason to suppose that the reliquary was more than a small casket. It is surely inconceivable that the reliquary could have been located on top of the reredos, the only other possible location, as it would scarcely have been visible at that height.' [11]

He also addresses the accessibility and function of the shrine-base for the pilgrim to St Davids,

'Assuming then, that the reliquary normally stood on the mensa there were two possibilities for veneration. Some, presumably under supervision, could come into the presbytery and prostrate themselves within the niches below the mensa. More readily accessible were the round-headed niches on the north side of the monument, into which pilgrims might again be able to insert their heads, not being able to see the shrine, but knowing at least that they had got as near as possible.

As has long been recognised, the dish-like recesses behind the quatrefoil openings were probably intended for monetary offerings. They are unusual - no other extant shrine appears to possess such features. Being on the feretory side of the monument, rather than the presumably more accessible aisle side, they are perhaps unlikely to have been accessible to pilgrims for much of the time.' [12]

---

11   John Crook.

12   John Crook.

In addition to monetary offerings, the pilgrim, like any modern tourist, would be encouraged to invest in the local economy: - *'Been there, done that, got the T-shirt'* - thus, when a medieval pilgrim visited a shrine one of the commonest mementos they might take home was a little cast lead badge which could be sewn onto their clothes or hat as an outward sign that they had completed their pilgrimage. Thousands of these pilgrim-badges are known from excavation or stray finds, but strangely none of the pilgrim-badges found in Pembrokeshire or elsewhere can be directly associated with the cult of St David.

Pilgrim badges, Pembrokeshire. Two are of Virgin and Child. Bottom row, left to right: bishop with crosier; St Thomas Becket; keys of St Peter, Rome; a king, possibly Edward the Confessor.

All this came to an end at the Reformation. The recently appointed bishop of St Davids, the fire-brand reformer William Barlow (whose protestant zeal during his incumbency as Prior of Haverfordwest had signally failed to endear him to the local population), seized the relics when they were brought out for display on St David's Day 1538,

'... I admonished the canons of Sainte Davids according to the kynges injunctions in no wyse to set forth fayned reliques for to allure people to supersticion, nether to advance the vayne observacion of unnecessary holy dayes abrogated by the kynges supreme authoritye, on sainte Davids daye the people wilfully solemnysinge the feest, certean reliques were set forth which I caused to be sequestered and taken awaye, detayninge them in my custody untill I maye be advertised of your lordships pleasour.'

Bishop Barlow described these *'fayned reliques'* as follows in his letter to Thomas Cromwell,

'...two heedes of sylver plate enclosinge two rotten skulles studded with putrified clowtes; Item, two arme bones, and a worme eaten boke covered with sylver plate.' [13]

The presence of two heads and two arm bones (since Edward I had taken one of St David's arms in 1284) implies that relics of two individuals were being displayed - probably St David and St Caradog. Since gospel books associated with early Celtic saints were amongst the relics revered in the pre-Norman cultural milieu it is possible that the *'worme eaten boke covered with sylver plate'* was an early illuminated manuscript like the Gospels of St Chad or the Book of Kells.

Some part of the materials associated with the shrine may have been concealed at this time - probably more in the hope that the political and religious wind might change than for personal profit - since in 1540 the Welsh Council headed by Lord Ferrers was required

'...to examine what jewels have been embezzled from the shrine of St Davids, and to put what remain in surety to the King's use.'

and six years later a reward of £40 was paid to James Leach as compensation for his pains in recovering *'plate and jewels which did belong to St. David's shrine in Wales.'* Whether the plate and jewels recovered by Leach were included in the valuation of 1544 is unclear, but at that time the Court of Augmentations calculated that *'the price of the sepulchre called le shryne of St David in Wales was £66 13s 4d.'* - a round figure of 100 marks.

The question arises - since the reliquary itself was clearly taken and destroyed at this time - whether Bishop Barlow also destroyed the architectural shrine-base, and whether what remains is a recreation dating from the reign of Mary Tudor.

An anonymous post-Reformation description of St David's Shrine survives from the later sixteenth century, and this provides strong circumstantial evidence that the shrine-base itself survived intact. At that time not only did it still support a painted canopy, but it bore three paintings in the south-facing niches, one of which was sufficiently old to be described as *'somewhat defaced.'*

'Over against these two Coffins [of Bishops Iorwerth and Anselm], on the other Side, is St. David's Shrine, between two Pillars of the Chancel, within a fair Arch of Timber-work painted. St David himself is painted in his Pontificalibus; and on each Side of him, is a Bishop Saint; one by the Inscription, is known to be St.Patrick; the other is somewhat defac'd.'

Browne Willis's *Survey* of 1717 drew upon this eye-witness account, stating that at this time,

---

13   From Wright, T.,(ed.), 1843. 'Letters Relating to the Suppression of the Monasteries', Camden Soc., 26. p.184, quoted in R. Morris, 'Cathedrals and Abbeys of England and Wales', Dent, 1979, p.165

A SHRINE RESTORED

'On the North Side of the Chancel, near the Steeple, under an Arch, is St. David's Tomb. Formerly it was all of one flat Stone, which is now broken into several Pieces; Above it, were anciently three Images; St David's in the Middle, St Patrick's on the right Hand, and St. Dennis's on the left, as Tradition informs us.'

The painted image of the third bishop, identified by Browne Willis as St Dennis, is intriguing. When King Henry VIII declared himself head of the English Church, the cult of St Thomas of Canterbury - a saint who was martyred for defending the rights of the church and the pope against King Henry II - was anathematised. His shrine at Canterbury was destroyed, his images throughout the country were broken, his feast day was no longer celebrated, and in Mass books of the period the rituals and music associated with his feast was torn out, defaced or crossed out with red ink.

In several instances wall paintings of St Thomas were simply converted into representations of other saints - like St Dennis or St Indracht - who had also had the top of their heads removed by non-medically qualified operatives. If our third painting at St Davids were one of these images of Becket damaged in the 1530s it would be clear evidence for a pre-1538 date for the paintings. However, the mere fact that the image had existed long enough to be 'somewhat defaced' is strong evidence for a medieval date, and it certainly could not have survived if the shrine-base had been taken down and re-erected in the mid-sixteenth century.

The Dean and Chapter of St Davids were in dispute with their Bishop in 1538 over other issues, and it seems highly likely that they stood firm against him and defied any attempt to remove the shrine base itself. Indeed Barlow saw the only way to abolish the cult of St David as being the removal of the See to Carmarthen (an exercise in which he was fortunately unsuccessful), complaining that he was unable to prevent

'...the manifold occasions of idolatrous infidelity and papistical practices (notwithstanding compulsory inhibitions and tongue professions)'

- presumably received from his subordinates at St Davids.

Even as late as 1571 residual allegiance to the old ways was evidently present at St Davids, since in that year Elis ap Howel, the cathedral's sexton,

'...of long tyme did conceall certain vngodly popish books: as masse books, hympnalls, Grailes, Antiphonrs, and such like (as it were looking for a day): Mr Chantor deprvid hym of the sextenship and the ffees thereunto belonging, Jn the p[rese]ns of mr Richard Ed chauncellor and other &c. And the said mr Chanter on the....day of this instant July, caused the said ungodly books to be canceld and torne in pieces in the Vestrie before his face, In the p[rese]ns of mr Chancello & other vt supra. &c.'

In the seventeenth century the choir aisles and the eastern chapels were unroofed, exposing the north face of the shrine base to the weather - hence the extent of the nineteenth century repair which was necessary during George Gilbert Scott's restoration. At this time the choir arcades were walled up, and the shrine-base became the support for the blocking of its arch.

At the inception of the shrine project a detailed archaeological survey of the physical fabric of the shrine base was undertaken to glean as much evidence as possible about its history, in order to inform the development of the project.

In the past, previous commentators have suggested that the mixed geology of the shrine-base - the incorporation of yellow Dundry stone in the lilac Caerfai stone structure - was evidence for later rebuilding. However, the use of Dundry stone for carving block was common in the thirteenth century and the builders would always have intended to paint the structure, so that the contrasting colours of the stonework would never have been intended to have shown.

Dundry stone was regarded as a high-quality carving stone in the late twelfth and thirteenth century, being exported as far afield as Ireland, and it was used at Glastonbury Abbey for fine carved work in the rebuilding following the disastrous fire of 1184, at Wells Cathedral for about a third of the figure sculptures on the west front (c.1235-42), and at Haverfordwest St Mary for the mid-thirteenth century north nave arcade and its finely carved capitals.

During the survey accurate archaeological elevation drawings were prepared. The shrine was particularly difficult to draw, since it barely contains a right-angle and the only true vertical line is the north-western corner (rebuilt by Scott in the 1860s). The structure stands on the sloping ground of the presbytery, and in places follows the slope, while in others the builders seem to have used a level to establish a true horizontal line.

The results of the survey lead to the conclusion that the building of the shrine was undertaken in two phases. The north elevation of the shrine-base is supported by the presence of round-headed arches in the lower register of the structure. These occur nowhere else on the shrine, and while round- and pointed-arches occur together in the somewhat earlier architecture of the nave, the semi-circular form is altogether out of place (even in west Wales) by the 1270s or 80s.[14] This raises the possibility that the builders of the 1275-84 shrine-base were reusing parts of its predecessor in the new structure - perhaps both in order to show respect to the old shrine and to hallow the new monument by incorporating material made sacred by its long proximity to the relics.

---

14   The recesses associated with the round-headed arches appear not to be related to the southern elevation when viewed in section.

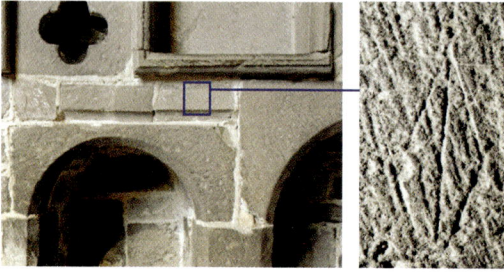

Also suggestive of this possible incorporation of earlier fabric is the only mason's mark on the shrine - a mark, rather like a signature, made by the mason who cut the block. I have not yet found this man's work anywhere else at St Davids and, while it is not a unique design, it is interesting that a very similar mark occurs at Wells Cathedral on parts of the building erected around 1180, and certainly before 1184. Did this man come to South Wales from Somerset when Bishop De Leia began the rebuilding of St Davids Cathedral in the 1180s? The stone on which this mark occurs is one of two with a moulded lower edge, which seem out of place in their present location, and which also argues for reuse from a previous structure.

That there was a pre-1275 shrine-base is also suggested by the architecture of the choir and presbytery. In the 1860s an arch containing a viewing oculus was discovered in the east wall behind the high altar. George Gilbert Scott recorded the discovery and speculated on its significance in a letter to Edward Freeman written on St David's Day 1866,

'We made a curious discovery under the great window now blocked up by Bishop Vaughan's Chapel. You will remember a mark as if of a doorway below that window in the Chapel, looking as if it opened in upon the back of the High Altar. We opened this and found it to be a deep arched recess some 2ft 6 or 3 ft from the floor and going perhaps 2/3 rds through the wall. At the back of it is a large and highly enriched cross in a recessed circle something like those in the triforium of the nave. The space between the arms of the cross being pierced through into the church a small recess behind the altar reaching to it from within. Around this larger cross are four other ornamented crosses on the surface. It must have been, I suppose, a place through which persons could peep through from without, perhaps at the shrine of St David.

Strangely enough, in the wall which blocked this recess were human bones carefully stowed away - Qu. Were these the bones of St. David taken out of his shrine in Henry VIII time?' [15]

Made before the eastern chapels were built and stylistically predating the existing shrine-base, this oculus, placed centrally behind the high altar at a comfortable viewing height, would have enabled pilgrims outside the east end of the choir to look into the church, and the question immediately arises (as it did to Scott) as to what they were looking at.

---

15   Letter G.G. Scott to E.A. Freeman, (coincidentally dated) 1 March 1866, John Rylands University Library, Manchester, FA1/1/150. Reproduced by courtesy of the University Library & Director, The John Rylands Library, The University of Manchester.

The east end of the church as rebuilt by Bishop Peter de Leia in the late twelfth century was planned with the choir stalls standing beneath the crossing, giving the presbytery an unusual length - considerably longer than the choir itself. The fifteenth century choir stalls are entirely contained within the crossing piers, and even with the bishop's throne and pulpit to the east the presbytery screen lies only halfway across the eastern bay of the choir, leaving three and a half bays of the four bay choir to be occupied by the presbytery. This extensive ritual space, now housing the Shrine of St David and the tomb of Edmund Tudor in its western bay and the high altar against the east wall, feels empty and over-large, it seems highly likely that it was originally intended to house the shrine of St David in its natural position of honour behind the high altar. With the high altar standing in the second bay, the shrine, orientated with its long axis east-west, would have occupied the east bay, and this was surely the focus of the viewing oculus in the east wall.

It was noticed during the fabric survey that incorporated in the masonry of the shrine on the north side are several fragments of tile, and if these proved not to be medieval it might indicate that there had been later rebuilding at high level. However, when Des Harries took out the later pointing before the new rendering was applied, it was clear that not only were the tiles medieval, but rather than being encaustic tiles with impressed designs typical of the thirteenth century and later, these tiles would appear to have been of the earlier green glazed type typical of the late twelfth century - just the sort which would have been available to the 1275 builders in the way of architectural salvage. Thus, rather than being indicative of post-medieval rebuilding these fragments support the view that the shrine-base remains essentially complete and undisturbed.

A diligent search was made for any traces of the three painted figures of bishops known to have graced the upper tier of arched recesses on the south elevation. At the back of the central niche there is a remnant of what may be the plaster ground and pale buff background of the image of St David, but none of the detail of the painting itself has survived, and elsewhere in these niches the stonework appears depressingly clean of such traces.

That the 'fair arch of Timberwork painted' was a projecting arched canopy standing on top of the shrine-base can be seen from the damage to the capitals of the

A SHRINE RESTORED

arcade to either side above the shrine. The position and form of these two area of breakage is identical to the damage caused to the capitals by accommodating the projecting curved timber canopy above the late fifteenth or early sixteenth century sedilia on the south side of the presbytery.

These scars on the capitals indicate that the medieval canopy was taller than its modern renewal, but it quickly became clear during the design process that replicating the original height would have detracted from the new images of the central register of the south elevation. The existing top of the shrine-base is an entirely Victorian creation, and there is no certainty as to the position of the original top of the masonry structure.

I have worked on the archaeology of cathedrals since 1978 and, while many of the projects I have participated in have produced exciting results - reconstructing the medieval colour schemes of the west fronts of Wells and Salisbury cathedrals, working out the order of construction of the thirteenth century building projects at Glastonbury Abbey and Wells Cathedral, and the west front, Porth-y-Twr and cloister projects here at St Davids Cathedral, for instance - none of these have truly incorporated the spiritual aspect which lies at the core of the enhancement of St David's Shrine, the ancient heart of Christianity in Wales.

I also want to say thank you to the people who instigated, designed and carried out this work. It has been a delight to work with you all and to see the magnificent product which has emerged from all your hard work. "Be joyful, keep the faith, do the little things" - I have been honoured to do a few of the little things towards this holy work.

The icons of the shrine: a rationale

The medieval Shrine of St David included paintings of three saints: St David, St Patrick and a third figure which was either that of St Andrew or St Denys of France. Given the dedication of the Cathedral it has been felt that St Andrew would be the most appropriate third figure for the restored shrine. It has also been suggested that two local saints closely connected with St David and the Cathedral should be portrayed on the back of the shrine: St Non (mother of St David) and St Stinan or Justinian, whose relics were originally preserved in the shrine along with those of St David.

Icons are a particularly appropriate form for the portrayal of these saints. Icons are sometimes described as 'windows into heaven'. They represent a meeting-point between the Church on earth and the Church in heaven: that numinous intersection of time and eternity which many pilgrims and visitors become aware of in our Cathedral. The gold-leaf background to an icon is not mere decorative gilding. It represents the uncreated light of heaven ('In that heavenly country bright, know they no created light', as the hymn-writer William Dix put it).

One of the most powerful expressions of the Communion of Saints of which icons are a visible expression comes at the beginning of the greatest modern Welsh poem about St David: 'Dewi Sant' by David Gwenallt Jones:

> 'Nid oes ffin rhwng deufyd yn yr Eglwys;
> Yr un ydyw'r Eglwys filwriaethus ar y llawr
> A'r Eglwys fuddugoliaethus yn y nef.
> A bydd y saint yn y ddwy-un Eglwys...'

> Translation:
> 'There is no border between two worlds in the Church;
> the Church militant on earth and the
> victorious Church in heaven are the same.
> And the saints shall be in the two-one Church...'

Eastern Orthodox icons follow a set 'canon'. That is to say that there are particular rules for the way in which each saint should be portrayed. Of the five saints depicted in the shrine there is obviously a long tradition of icons of St Andrew, while the Brotherhood of St Seraphim of Sarov at Walsingham has a fairly well established icon of 'St Patrick Enlightener of Ireland'. Two rather different icons of St David/Dewi Sant have come from the Orthodox Church at Blaenau Ffestiniog and the Brotherhood of St Seraphim of Sarov.

However, as St Davids is the Mother Church of the people of Wales, it was felt that the Cathedral should have the freedom to create its own particular icons for the national shrine, rather than follow canons established by others.

St David

David is believed to have been born at the beginning of the 6th century. According to legend and other sources he is believed to be of a noble family; after becoming a priest he was to found several monasteries until he finally settled at Mynyw or Menevia. There in 'Glyn Rhosyn' he led a life of extreme asceticism which was modelled on that of Egyptian monks. In 560 he is believed to have attended the Synod at Brefi (now known as Llanddewi Brefi) where due to the eloquence and power of his words he was chosen to be primate of the Cambrian Church. In his 'Life' written by Rhigyfarch he is believed to have gone on pilgrimage to Jerusalem where he was consecrated as Archbishop by the patriarch there. Upon his deathbed he left his followers with these words: "Be joyful, keep the faith and do the little things" which remain an inspiration to Christians in Wales and throughout the world today. David was canonised by Pope Calixtus II in 1120 and it was Archbishop Arundel in 1398 who ordered that his feast day be kept on the 1st of March.

David is depicted in the icon as a comparatively young man, clean-shaven, with a Celtic tonsure. This in itself is a stark contrast to the typical images of David which see him as an old man in episcopal dress. His robes are similar to those of the order of Egyptian monks which influenced St David. Drapery in icons is painted so that it hints at the spiritual state of the body beneath. The robe on St David's icon is highlighted at the points where the robe touches the body of the saint. As a Celtic saint, the head of St David is shaven and reveals a high forehead (tonsure).

The Celtic knot brooch, which holds St David's robe together, is taken from the Abraham Stone which can be found at Pen Arthur in St Davids. It is dated to the 11th century and marks the graves of Hedd and Isaac, the sons of Bishop Abraham who were murdered by Danish raiders in 1080.

St David is seen holding a Gospel Book in one hand and the other is raised in blessing (as befitting a Bishop of the Church). The style of the lettering found on this icon and the others is influenced by The Book of Kells.

The vision of St David as depicted in this icon is of a man at the height of his powers, representing the present - interpreting the Word through the power of the Holy Spirit as he brings its message to Wales.

St Andrew

St Andrew was an apostle, martyr and brother of Simon Peter. He was a fisherman by trade whose home was in Capernaum. He was a follower of John the Baptist, before becoming an apostle of Christ. His name is amongst the first four of the apostles in the Gospels and he is specially mentioned for his role in the feeding of the five thousand. Tradition states that he was crucified in the year 60 at Patras, in Achaia. He is the patron saint of Scotland, Greece and Russia and co-patron of the Cathedral. His feast day falls on 30th of November.

Andrew is depicted with a saltier cross (X), which can be seen behind Andrew in the newly restored shrine. The inscription on St Andrew's scroll reads 'We have found the Messiah' and is taken from John 1:41. Icon-writer Sara Crisp says:

"The painting of an icon requires identification with a tradition. It is always copied from a prototype, the same image having been painted many times over the centuries. This is the format for the icon of St Andrew where a prototype already exists."

St Andrew is shown as an older, bearded figure. He represents the past, not as something dead, but rather as a living tradition rooted in the faith and teaching of the Apostles.

St Patrick

St Patrick is believed to have been born in Wales during the early part of the 5th century. Patrick was brought up as a Christian but at the age of sixteen he was captured by Irish pirates and spent six years as a herdsman in Ireland. Upon his escape and return to Britain he underwent training for the Christian ministry, obtaining an excellent knowledge of the Latin Bible. He soon departed to become 'bishop in Ireland' and he spent the rest of his life there. His feast day is the 17th of March.

St Patrick is depicted in similar Celtic attire to that of St David. He carries with him a staff to aid him on his missionary walk. St Patrick is depicted, as befitting the patron saint of Ireland, in a green robe, however it is lined in orange. This is symbolic of Patrick's patronage of the people of North and South Ireland and of the great reconciliation which has occurred between those peoples during the past fifteen years.

St Patrick represents the future, the future which the Gospel of Christ can bring to all people. Through his symbolic dress Patrick represents the power of Christian love, peace and reconciliation. He symbolises the hope and faith which can bring God's people through times of tribulation and distress.

St Non

Non lived in West Wales and was seduced by Sant, the prince of Ceredigion. Through this relationship she gave birth to a son: Dewi Sant or St David. Tradition states that this was her only child however other sources argue that she had two daughters, Mor and Magna. She is believed to have moved to Brittany, where her cult is centered on Dirinon. It was there that she was buried. Her feast day is the 5th of March.

The icon of St Non is based upon a medieval carving depicting St Non holding the infant St David which is similar to typical portrayals of the Blessed Virgin Mary. The medieval carving was originally from Capel Non in Llan-non and is now held in the Ceredigion museum.

Non's robes are decorated with gold and include a repeated cross design from The Book of Kells. In her left arm she bears the infant St David and in her right hand she holds a cross. The shape of this Celtic Cross can be found on a stone near St Non's Well.

St Justinian

St Justinian was a hermit and martyr who resided on Ramsey Island, Pembrokeshire. He was Breton by birth and lived a solitary life on the island of Ramsay. Tradition states that Justinian was decapitated by his servants who were disheartened with his strict regime, and according to folklore he carried his severed head, across the waters, to the place where he wished to be buried and where a church was later built in his honour.

Justinian is depicted as a man of prayer and as an ascetic (which was the reason for his decapitation). He too bears a staff to aid him on his missionary endeavours. In line with the customs of icon painting as St Justinian's left hand is neither undertaking a blessing nor holding an object it is covered by his robes.

THE CANOPY OF THE SHRINE AND ITS THEOLOGICAL MEANING

The painted oak canopy was made by Friend Wood to designs by Peter Bird and seeks to replicate an original 13th century construction.

Traditionally canopies were built over the tombs of saints and above altars. Canopies serve to remind us of the closeness of the heavenly places to us here on earth. The main part of the canopy is painted in medieval colours and decorated with gold stars to represent the heavens.

The white roses joining the ribs of the canopy represent the beauty of the Gospel, which holds together both heaven and earth, and reminds us that this valley is known as 'Glyn Rhosyn' meaning Vale of the Rose.

Eleven wood carvings at the top of the canopy relate to different aspects of the lives of the saints depicted in the icons beneath them:

Shamrock

The shamrock was used by St Patrick to teach his followers the Christian doctrine of the Holy Trinity: Father, Son and Holy Spirit. It is also the emblem of the Irish people and has deep Christian origins.

White Hart

The carving of the white hart depicts a legend relating to St Patrick and his followers who, when being persecuted by Irish druids, were protected mystically and transformed into deer.

Snake

This carving refers to the ancient legend of St Patrick expelling all snakes from the emerald isle and also represents his banishing of paganism from Ireland.

Daffodil

The daffodil is a Victorian symbol and is, along with the leek, a national emblem of Wales. Since Victorian times the daffodil has been worn traditionally by women on St David's Day. The triple headed daffodil in the canopy reminds us of St David's faithfulness to the teaching of the Trinity.

Bell & Staff

The staff symbolises St David's authority as a bishop and shepherd over the Welsh people. The bell, known as St David's 'bangu', is a Celtic bell and was probably used in the context of the liturgy. This carving reminds us of St David's role as the father of Christianity in Wales.

Scallop Shell

The scallop shell, also known as the pilgrim's shell, is an ancient symbol of pilgrimage and baptism used by pilgrims on their journeys to centres of pilgrimage such as St Davids.

Water

St David was known as 'Dewi Dyfrwr' meaning 'David the Water Man.' This refers to David's ascetic monasticism, which only permitted the drinking of water, and to his work as a missionary which led to the baptising of many. It also reminds us of the practice during St David's time of standing in cold running water whilst meditating and reciting the psalms.

Leek

The leek, like the daffodil, is also a national emblem of Wales. According to legend, St David ordered his soldiers on the eve of a battle with the Saxons to identify themselves by wearing the vegetable on their helmets. This old tradition is still remembered today when Welshmen wear a leek on St David's Day.

Loaves & Fishes

St Andrew, the brother of St Peter, is represented by the carving of loaves and fishes. Two fish and four loaves are depicted in this carving, reminding us of the feeding of the five thousand. The fifth loaf of bread is missing and serves to remind us that Jesus is the 'Bread of Life' on whom we all feed.

Ship

The ship depicted in this wood-carving reminds us that the church, like a ship, helps the Christian sail through the difficult waters of life. It was also at the sea of Galilee that St Andrew had his first meeting with Jesus. St Andrew is also the patron saint of fishermen.

Thistle

The thistle is the national symbol of Scotland. It serves to remind us that St Andrew is the patron saint of Scotland and shares joint patronage of this Cathedral with St David.

The niches

Three niches, formerly for kneeling at the foot of the shrine, can be found at the front of the shrine. Two reliquaries, reputed to contain the remains of St David and St Justinian, can be found in the outer niches whilst a replica of a Celtic 'Bangu' bell graces the central niche. The replica bell was kindly donated to the cathedral by the 128th Bishop of St Davids, The Right Reverend Wyn Evans. Commenting on his gift the Bishop said:

"Portable Altar, Pastoral Staff, Gospel Book and Hand Bell: these were the relics of their founding saints treasured by the great churches and monasteries of early mediaeval Western Britain. The community which bore the name of the saint did not look to the tomb or the corporeal relics of the saint for the authentication and guarantee of its power status and possessions. It was rather to the smaller relics made or used by the saint during his or her ministry.

These objects were believed to wield the miraculous powers of their original owners, and they were used to guarantee the sanctions and oaths were sworn on them before God and the saint on the altar. Many of them had particular names: St Padarn's staff was called Curwen and Giraldus Cambrensis tells us that St David's hand bell was called 'Bangu'.

St David had other relics beside 'Bangu': in the middle ages, his relics were to be found at the major churches associated with him: his Pastoral Staff at Llanddewi Brefi; his portable altar at Llangyfelach; his Gospel Book at St Davids and his Bell at Glasgwm. Not one of these have survived to the present day.

When I came into post, the sculptor David Petersen kindly made a replica of 'Bangu' for me, based on the many examples of the bells of Celtic saints which have survived in Britain and Ireland. It now graces the refurbished shrine."

A SHRINE RESTORED

22

The craftmanship

How the icons were made

There are two main styles of icon painting, namely classic Byzantine and Early Italian. The same materials and procedures are used but the way of modelling form is slightly different. Byzantine icon painting uses highly stylised and stepped highlighting where the edges between tones are not blended as seen in Greek and Russian icons. Early Italian and northern European painting has subtle blending between the tones and is softer and more naturalistic. A combination of both styles has been used for the icons at St David's Shrine.

In order to paint the icons Sara Crisp, following techniques dating back to the Byzantine period, painted with egg tempera on gessoed wooden panels. Well-seasoned solid lime wood panels were used for the icons, as canvas is too flexible to hold the egg tempera and gesso, and these were constructed by Dunstan Commander. The wood is produced as narrow planks and therefore they have to be clamped together and joined by interlocking dovetails. Two wooden spleens are slotted in the back and these spleens allow for slight movement of the wood with the passage of time and are fitted without glue or screws.

The boards were first sized with warm rabbit skin glue and then left to dry. The muslin was then glued to the board with the same hot glue, covering the front and sides of the board. After twenty-four hours the cloth was trimmed and corners were neatly rasped and filed.

The gesso mixture was then applied to the linen. Gesso is a mixture of chalk whiting and rabbit skin glue (whiting is natural calcium carbonate) and was applied whilst still warm over the muslin on the icon panel in a series of approximately 15-18 thin coats with thirty minutes drying time between coats. This was then sanded to give an absolutely flawless finish (like porcelain).

At this stage the gesso was incised with a sharp 3-edged stylus, creating a border around the three large panels. The use of a border is common in illuminated manuscripts and gospels of the time. A line drawing of the saint was then incised into the gesso ($1/3$ mm deep). The background was then prepared for gilding.

A soft clay called 'bole', mixed with gelatine, was applied to the gesso. This acts as a 'cushion' for the gold leaf. It was painted directly on to the gesso then smoothed with wire wool, wet-and-dry sandpaper and finally polished with a velvet cloth so its appearance is that of polished mahogany. Using a small piece of agate the gold was then burnished leaving the appearance of solid gold. Decorative patterns and indenting into the gold were also done at this stage whilst the clay was still damp.

The image on the icon was painted in a series of several coats. The pigments used are gritty dry powder, ground with a muller on a glass slab and mixed daily with egg yolk (which acts as a binder) and cold purified water (which was taken from St Non's Well).

Friend Wood reflects on the creation of the canopy

My job is to turn ideas, words and drawings into reality – a three dimensional structure, in this case made from oak. The previous Cathedral Architect, the late Peter Bird, determined the proportions and position of the canopy in relation to the shrine and the two pillars. The top of the shrine slopes in two directions and dips in the centre. Therefore full size patterns and many measurements were taken, especially of the two pillars. A full size drawing of the cross section was also made. Full size mock ups were made from softwood and were used in the early site visits and discussions to enable final decisions to be made on the finer points of the design.

I would have been delighted to have used local materials, however my main concern was ensured quality in the long lengths required. My trusted supplier delivered some excellent oak, which to my surprise came from Hungary. Although I use machines to saw and plane the planks to size I still do a lot of traditional hand-work which requires a lot of physical effort. The Cathedral is a truly wonderful and inspiring space to work in and it was a joy to work with a team of thoughtful and appreciative individuals.

A shadow gap of 6mm was required between the woodwork and stone pillars, so several day fittings were required to mark and fit as necessary. There is an excellent book 'The Art and Nature of Workmanship' by David Pye in which he describes the workmanship of risk which applies to most of my work. Care and concentration is required throughout the many processes to create the envisioned final form. Most prototypes, that is the first of a new design, "grow" in an organic form of design.

After the challenge to mind and body which is the making, comes the finishing. All outer surfaces need to be cleaned up with smoothing plane or scraper. The south frame and panels were coated with rabbit skin glue, to seal the wood then many coats of egg tempera to build up the finish, all under the guidance of Sara Crisp. All other surfaces of the canopy were limed.

With help from Jerry Sampson and Steve Wilson the patterae designs were developed, along with the rose for the bosses. The rose bosses were painted and guilded by Sara and Steve.

The curved panels of the south side were shaped to match the curved ribs. Each panel was marked out with stars from the architect Henry Bird's patterns. The stars were incised, rabbit skin glue sized, coated with gesso, bole and then double guilded. Really a challenge to one's mind, with so much repetition, as well as the workmanship of risk and the level of skill required. The result is beyond our wildest dreams. At every stage the supportive comments and appreciation were sustaining and created a good working atmosphere.

During the final weeks and days all the separate components came together on and in the shrine – an amazing experience for all of us. The qualities of these materials compliment each other and create a truly awesome overall material, visual and ultimately spiritual emotion.

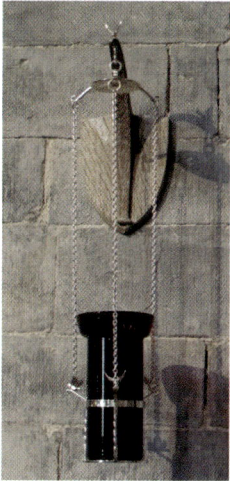

The rationale & creation of the vigil lamp

A vigil lamp is often lit in front of an icon, or in the case of the Shrine of St David, several icons, because it reminds us of Christ. Jesus said: 'I am the light of the world' (John 8.12) and so the light of the vigil lamp reminds us of that light by which Christ illumines our souls. Secondly the lamp is lit to remind us of the radiant character of the saint, or several saints, for saints are called 'sons of light' (John 12.36).

The lamp is made from Sterling Silver and the base and top cap are made from sheet, the band is made from rectangular wire and all other parts (except the doves) are made from round wire.

Firstly in order to create the lamp the base and top were sawn from a square piece of sheet and filed into shape. The top was then domed to create a cap. The horizontal band was cut to length, shaped and soldered to fit the glass lamp.

Each vertical arm began as round wire which was rolled slightly to give a flat surface before being twisted at the centre. The ends were then splayed and scrolled to accommodate the doves. The chain-holding arms on the top cap were formed in a similar way, without the twist, and shaped to sit snugly on the cap. Each arm was then carefully soldered into place. The chain was made from the same round wire, which was drawn down to a smaller diameter. The wire was then wound by hand to make each link, which was individually soldered to make up the chain.

A dove was made from several pieces of sheet soldered together to make a block which was then sawn and filed to make the main body and head of the dove. The wings, made from a further piece of sheet, were shaped and soldered onto the body. Because of the difficulty in making four identical doves, the original, hand-made dove, was used as a master-pattern for producing a mould so that identical castings could be formed. These were then hand finished, before soldering them into position.

The lamp holder was then decorated with hand-engraving around the edge of the base and the underside of the cap, where the un-engraved area forms a star which echoes the stars in the canopy of the shrine. The lamp has been hallmarked in Birmingham where a special mark was also added to it to commemorate The Queen's Diamond Jubilee. This is particularly fitting as HM Queen Elizabeth II is a member of The Chapter of the Cathedral.

THE SHRINE APPEAL

In September 2010 the Dean of St Davids Cathedral at the Friends Festival launched the Appeal to restore the Shrine of St David. In order to achieve this, he appointed seven shrine guardians to assist him in this important project. Over the course of several months Mr Arwel Davies, Mrs Stephanie Halse, Miss Llywela Harris, Miss Moyra Skenfield, The Revd Canon Dorrien Davies, The Revd Canon Chancellor Patrick Thomas, The Revd Harri Williams and the Dean met to discuss fundraising ideas, design options and other matters relating to the restoration of the Shrine. During the course of the appeal, which lasted some 18 months, over £100,000 was raised by donations and sponsorship. One of the most successful campaigns of the appeal was the 'Sponsor a Star' scheme which enabled individuals or groups to sponsor one of the 189 stars in the canopy of the Shrine. In addition to this the various symbols on the canopy were sponsored by individuals, as were the roses, and the icons on the front of the Shrine were dedicated in memory of individuals who had contributed considerably to the life of the Cathedral.

the friends OF ST DAVIDS CATHEDRAL

SHRINE APPEAL

Please show your generous support and help us raise £150,000 to restore the Shrine of St David

The icon of St David is dedicated to the memory of Mr Peter Bird. Peter served for many years as the Cathedral Architect and was responsible for the initial drawings of the restored shrine. His untimely death in 2011 left a tremendous void in the life of the Cathedral and of the firm he had devoted his life to: Caroe & Partners.

The icon of St Andrew is dedicated to the memory of Mr Ray Tarr. Ray served as Secretary of the Friends of St Davids Cathedral from 1988-2007 and was also responsible for the guided tours offered in the Cathedral to visitors. He died in 2008 and as St Andrew is the patron saint of the Guild of Stewards and Welcomers in the Cathedral, it was felt fitting that his memorial should be attached to this icon.

The icon of St Patrick is dedicated to the memory of Mr Odo Saunders and Mrs Catherine Saunders. Odo served as a Headmaster of the Church School in St Davids and his wife also worked as a teacher in the school. Catherine was also a committed member of the Welsh congregation who worship in the Lady Chapel.

A Shrine Restored

The Dedication of the Shrine of St David

Mrs Jennie Kitchell, Canon Chancellor Patrick Thomas, the Canon Residentiary & the Secretary at Oriel y Parc

The procession proceeds through the city

The procession arriving at the Cathedral

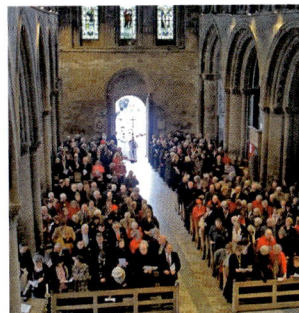

The service begins

On the 1st of March 2012 the Shrine of St David was restored to the glory of God.

The day began with a procession from Oriel y Parc through the streets of the City.

The icon of St David was borne through the streets by the Canon Residentiary.

The procession was led by the Canons' Verger, followed by the Guardians of the Shrine, members of the Cathedral Chapter, the Honorary Assistant Bishop, the Dean and the Bishop of St Davids.

At midday the procession stopped on the Cross Square in order that the Bishop of St Davids might bless the city, diocese and the nation.

The procession then continued down towards the Cathedral, arriving at the West Door just before 12.30pm.

At 12.30pm the Eucharist began with the uplifting hymn by Bishop Timothy Rees 'Arglwydd trefni mewn doethineb.'

Over 500 people were in attendance at the service.

The Bishop celebrated the Eucharist with dignity and solemnity, and was assisted by: The Revd Benjamin Rabjohns (Assistant Curate of the Rectorial Benefice of Aberavon) as Deacon and The Revd Gareth Reid (Assistant Curate of the Rectorial Benefice of Dewisland) as Sub-Deacon.

The Bishop reminded the congregation that events such as this only happen every 750 years or so!

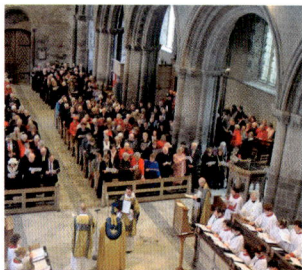

The Bishop leads the congregation in worship

The Deacon proclaims the Gospel

The Bishop at the High Altar

The Bishop and Shrine Guardians before the Shrine

The Dedication of the Shrine

Following the Dean's Sermon the Choir and Sanctuary Party processed to the High Altar during the offertory whilst the hymn 'For all the Saints' was sung. The Eucharist was celebrated at the High Altar and the communion setting for the occasion was Vierne's *Messe Solennelle*.

During the distribution of communion the choir sang Bruckner's *Locus Iste* and then during the singing of the post-communion hymn the Bishop, the Dean and the Shrine Guardians gathered around the newly restored shrine.

The Bishop then dedicated the Shrine with these words:

'Heavenly Father, as we stand before his Shrine at the heart of this cathedral church, we give thanks for your servant David and for all others who have kept the flame of faith alight in this sacred place across the centuries.

We pray for all the pilgrims who will visit David's Shrine.

May it be for them a focus of quiet reflection, where, in the secret places of their hearts, they may experience the truth of David's teaching: the joy of your creation, inspiring praise and worship; the faith of Christ, sustaining and strengthening in times of testing and adversity – and the desire to carry out transforming acts of loving kindness, empowered by your Spirit.

Within the Communion of Saints, uniting the church on earth and the church in heaven, we join our prayers with those of Andrew, Apostle and Fisherman of Souls, Patrick, son of Wales and Enlightener of Ireland, and David, the Christian guide and inspiration of our nation and people, as we dedicate this Shrine, in the name of the Father and of the Son and of the Holy Spirit. Amen.'

The Bishop then proceeded to anoint the Shrine whilst the choir sang the 'Te Deum'.

The service concluded with the Bishop bestowing God's blessing upon the congregation.

A SHRINE RESTORED

The Visit of the Archbishop of Canterbury

On Saturday the 24th of March 2012 the Cathedral was privileged to welcome The Most Rev'd and Right Honourable Dr Rowan Williams as the Celebrant and Preacher. Dr Williams, as Patron of the Appeal to restore the Shrine, had been following the developments in the Cathedral very closely and was determined to visit the Shrine at the earliest opportunity. The weather on that day was glorious and the Archbishop was joined in a celebration of the Eucharist by over 250 people. The Archbishop in his sermon reminded the congregation of the importance of the saints in pointing us to God and providing for us an example of holiness of living.

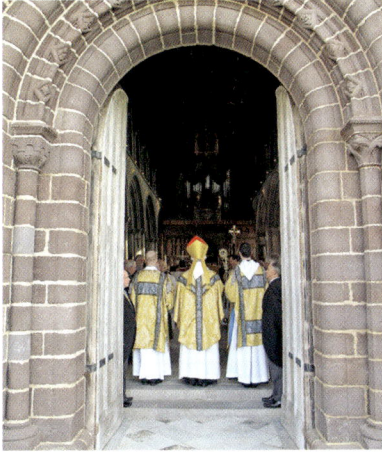

The Archbishop at the West Door of the Cathedral

The Archbishop delivering his address

The Archbishop of Canterbury with the Bishop, the Dean and members of the Cathedral Foundation.

The Archbishop of Canterbury at prayer in front of the shrine

Address given by The Very Revd Jonathan Lean at the Dedication of the Shrine of St David on 1ˢᵗ of March 2012

Today we gather together to celebrate the feast of Saint David, patron of this Cathedral and patron of this great nation of Wales. We gather together to honour a man, who throughout his life sought to follow our Lord and Saviour Jesus Christ. It was he, who as the Bishop and hymnist Timothy Rees wrote, 'strove and suffered here the holy Church to plant.' So that is why we gather together today, to honour him and to praise God for the gifts he bestows upon his Church in every generation. But David has left us more than a building in which to remember him; he has left us words of wisdom, words of faith: 'Be joyful, keep the faith, and do the little things.' These words have echoed down the centuries, have become part of the memory of the Welsh people and they are words which should encourage and inspire us today.

Being joyful seems to be an ever increasing challenge for the Church in this current age. With our divisions and disharmony, we seem to lack the joy of an Easter people, which is what we are called to be. The Church's purpose here on earth is to profess the faith of the crucified, risen and ascended Lord. To make known to all the world the honour of his name, and to make his love a reality in the lives of all God's people. As the psalmist encourages us today, we should rejoice in our faith in God and our hearts should be glad that we know and love him. David in his life sought to preach the joyful message of the Gospel to all people. He travelled the length and breadth of this nation and others in order to proclaim the salvation which was won for us by Jesus Christ. Today let us be joyful in our expression of faith, let us rejoice in our common witness and celebrate all that is good and wonderful and beautiful about our God.

To keep the faith, in this so called secular world, can seem to be a great challenge. When the Church is faced with increasing bureaucracy and legislation from the state, when the public expression of Christian values is being attacked, we may as followers of Christ find this a difficult task. Yet our Gospel reading today reminds us that following Jesus Christ in word and deed isn't an easy thing, or one to be taken lightly. We are called to take up our cross and follow him, we are called to make sacrifices in our lives so that we too may follow Jesus more nearly and love him more dearly. St David in his life did exactly that. He fought for the faith, in the face of opposition from those in power and authority, but it was through the strength of his teaching, and his holiness of living that he was able to convert their souls for Christ. So we too in our own age must seek to keep the faith handed to us by the Apostles and to stand firm, as St David did, for the truth of that despite what popular opinion may be.

To do the little things, what does that really mean? Well David in his life sought to provide us an example of Christian living. He sought through word and deed to make Christ known. Through the community which he founded here, based upon the principles of prayer, worship and hospitality he sought to reveal something of the glory of God, of the incarnate Christ. So we too in our day must seek through our lives to reflect Christ and to see his face in one another. We must seek to lay aside trivial and petty matters and always place Christ at the heart of what we do and who we are. We must do those little things, those acts of kindness and generosity which speak something of the love of God.

'Be joyful, keep the faith, and do the little things.' Those last few words left to us by St David should be inspirational for us today as we gather together to honour his life and to re-dedicate the Shrine which bears his name. The re-dedication of this Shrine is not about an aesthetic improvement to the building, it is not about honouring David more than God, rather it is about placing David's example of Christian life and witness at the heart of our Cathedral, and being inspired by him to follow God all the days of our life.

It is my hope and prayer that as we re-dedicate this shrine, so we will re-dedicate ourselves to the great commission of making new disciples. For this Shrine will place prayer, healing and pilgrimage at the heart of this Cathedral once again. It will offer each and every one of us a means of encountering God in many and varied ways. Through treading the pilgrim's path I trust that we will all experience something of the wonder and mystery of God and also experience what it truly is to follow in Christ's steps.

Today we gather together to honour St David and to re-dedicate his Shrine to the glory of God. The depiction of David found in this shrine, sees him clad in Celtic attire, with symbols of his Christian witness and ministry, but most importantly he is looking towards the High Altar. Towards that place where Christ is revealed to us in Word and Sacrament. This Shrine honours Saint David and his life, but let us pray today that it will help, encourage and inspire all who visit this place to confess, as St David did, that Jesus Christ is Lord and Saviour of us all. Let us pray that it will help each and every one of us to Be joyful, to keep the faith and to do the little things, and let us pray that today will mark the beginning of our great mission to turn visitors into pilgrims.

Address given by The Revd Canon Chancellor Patrick Thomas at the Choral Eucharist for the Feast of St Non on 4ᵗʰ of March 2012

Revelation 19.8: *'...the fine linen is the righteous deeds of the saints.'*

When Dean Jonathan asked me to become a Guardian of the Shrine of St David, my initial reaction was one of panic.

I couldn't say no, of course – but I feared that it meant that I was doomed to spend the rest of my ministry lurking somewhere in the vicinity of the shrine – keeping an eagle eye out for small children intent on scribbling on it – or foreign tourists hoping to chip off a chunk to take home as a souvenir – or even (and here my imagination went into Brother Cadfael mode) covetous canons from lesser cathedrals plotting to pinch a relic or two in the hope of establishing a shrine of their own.

But that initial panic quickly subsided – and was replaced by an increasing sense of awe and wonder at the privilege of being asked to care for a shrine that is both an extraordinary work of art – its icons being windows into heaven as icons are meant to be – and also a focus of prayer: a lasting reminder to pilgrims and visitors that this is a sacred space – one of the holiest places in the British Isles and indeed the whole of Christendom.

T.S. Eliot called Little Gidding 'a place where prayer has been valid', and the same is true of this Cathedral, sanctified by centuries of prayer. The restored shrine of St David will ensure that it continues to be a place of prayer for many centuries to come.

Gwenallt, one of our great Welsh religious poets, wrote about 'y ddwy-un eglwys' – 'the two-one church' made up of the victorious church in heaven and the church militant here on earth: the church in the timelessness of eternity and the church in the linear time of our human experience, bound together in a single communion of saints.

Gwenallt was aware of how each of the two elements of the communion of saints could inter-relate. He depicts St David stepping into the society of mid-twentieth century Wales, bringing the transforming message of the Gospel to our people, just as he had done fourteen centuries before – and there is a sense in which our restored shrine continues this process into the twenty-first century.

This morning we remember not only St David, but also St Non, his mother, whose feast day we keep today. St David's medieval biographer tells us that Non was a nun who was raped by a sixth century king of Ceredigion, which, given the rather brutal nature of much of Welsh life at that time, seems probable enough.

If we look behind the various legends that attached themselves to St Non in Welsh and Breton folklore, we glimpse a young woman from a deeply religious background, traumatized by an appalling experience, and then left to bring up her little son on her own.

And it's that relationship between the mother and her son which is profoundly significant. A recent survey showed that Christians in Britain are much worse than members of other religions at passing on their faith between the generations. I suspect that this may be something that has developed most markedly during the past half century.

Certainly I belong to a generation where it was not uncommon for mothers to teach their children the Lord's Prayer and other prayers as well. That was my own experience in a not particularly devout home. Mothers and grandmothers have played – and often still play – a crucial part in planting the seeds of Christian belief and practice in their children's or grandchildren's lives.

A wise and lovely old Polish lady in my former parish up in the hills once said to me: "Passing the faith to your children is like packing a suitcase for them. They leave home and wander off and may go in all sorts of directions. Perhaps they never open the suitcase at all. Perhaps one day they do open it and find what they really need within it. But what matters is that the suitcase is there. You have given it to them."

And what St Non passed on to her son David were those familiar words which David passed on to us, recorded in the early Welsh version of his life by the Anchorite of Llanddewibrefi: 'Byddwch lawen, cedwch eich ffydd a'ch cred, a gwnewch y pethau bychain a glywsoch ac a welsoch gennyf i.' 'Be joyful, keep your faith and your belief, and do the little things you've heard and seen from me.'

'Be joyful!' It was important to strike that note, if only because you don't have to be an expert in Welsh religious history to know that there have been periods when much of Welsh Christianity has seemed a dismal, dull, deadening and deadly affair.

Non's life must have been desperate enough at times – and yet she sang the psalms and canticles she'd learnt off by heart in the convent to her little son – and taught him the joy that comes through praise.

And that praise has echoed through the ages. There's the astonishing Welsh Benedicite in the Black Book of Carmarthen, verses which some scholars suggest may have been originally composed here in St Davids: 'Gogoneddog Arglwydd, henffych well!' 'Hail, glorious Lord! May church and chancel praise you, may chancel and church praise you...' And the praise expands to embrace the world, the cosmos, the tradition of faith and all human creativity.

That praise is continued by the great Welsh religious poets of the Middle Ages and by the hymn writers of eighteenth century Carmarthenshire, and it reaches a glorious climax in that wonderful hymn by Pembrokeshire's modern poet W. Rhys Nicholas which is so often sung to 'Pantyfedwen'. And of course that extraordinary tradition of praise is at the heart of the life and worship of this Cathedral: St David's own cathedral, so often filled with the most beautiful sacred music.

'Keep your faith and your belief' was St David's second command – which may seem uncomplicated enough in a country whose culture has been shaped by fifteen centuries of Christianity. But, as we're all very much aware, and as Dean Jonathan reminded us on St David's Day, life has changed. For many in Wales faith and belief are now things that they seem to find it only to easy to live without.

To my mind, the essence of faith is what remains when everything else is stripped away. It's that something that keeps us going when going on seems utterly impossible... That wounded hand that reaches out in love to grasp our hand in the deepest darkness and leads us gently forward into unexpected light.

Non must have known that: raped, abandoned, left to care for her little son all on her own – and yet, even in the worst times, her faith sustained her - and she passed it on to David.

And faith is linked to belief. Gwenallt, in his poem about St David, speaks of 'the saints, our oldest ancestors, who built Wales on the foundation of the crib, the cross and the empty grave': Incarnation, Crucifixion, Resurrection – the depth of God's love for us revealed in Jesus Christ, God come among us as one of us for our sake. That was the basis of the Gospel that Non taught David – and that David preached and that we preach still.

But there's a danger here: one that the fashionable opponents of religion are only too quick to remind us of. Belief can easily become a stick to beat others with, and faith can be perverted into fanaticism and end up planting bombs or firing bullets.

The antidote which gives faith and belief both depth and real meaning is that third command which David inherited from Non: 'do the little things...'

The 'little things' represent faith and belief lived out in everyday life through apparently insignificant but in fact hugely significant acts of loving-kindness. I don't know if Mother Teresa of Calcutta knew much about St David, but I do know that she was on the same wavelength as him when she said 'We can do no great things, only little things with great love.'

Non's gift to David was Our Lord's gift to her – and has become David's gift to us, his spiritual family in this corner of Wales: a faith expressed through joyful praise and a belief lived out through the small kindnesses that heal wounds and bring hope and enable the rich variety of humankind to live in harmony one with another.

That's the 'fine linen bright and pure' which St John the Divine speaks of in the words we heard from Revelation: the righteous deeds of the saints which clothe the church to make her a fitting bride for Christ.

The daily life of the shrine & Pilgrimage

The Shrine of St David is a focus for prayer, healing and pilgrimage within the life of the Cathedral. Prayers at the Shrine are held each Friday at 12.00pm. All are welcome to attend this service of prayer and reflection during which those present are invited to be anointed with holy oil at the shrine as a symbol of healing, reconciliation and consecration.

Groups are encouraged to come on pilgrimage to the Cathedral and further details about such opportunities can be obtained from the Deanery Office.

St David's Shrine Prayer

Heavenly Father, we thank you for Saint David,
the founder of our Christian community,
who taught and lived the Gospel in this valley.
Bless the restored Shrine of St David,
that it may become a source of comfort, hope and healing,
strengthening the faith and belief of pilgrims and visitors,
to the honour of your Son, our Saviour Jesus Christ. Amen.

Gweddi Creirfa Dewi Sant

Dad nefol, diolchwn i ti am Dewi Sant,
syflaenydd ein cymuned Gristnogol, a ddysgodd yr Efengyl
trwy ei eiriau a'i weithredoedd yma yng Nglyn Rhosyn.
Bendithia Creirfa adferedig Dewi Sant,
er mwyn iddi ddod â chysur, gobaith ac iachâd,
gan gryfhau ffydd a chred pererinion ac ymwelwyr,
er anrhydedd dy Fab, ein Gwaredwr Iesu Grist. Amen.

Biographies

Sara Crisp is from St Davids and is now based in Solva where she lives with her young family. She has been making icons for several years using egg-tempera and 24-carat gold leaf on gessoed wooden panels. In her icon painting she uses traditional methods and techniques dating back to the twelfth century. Icons invite the viewer to see not only the image of the saint depicted but also the spirit of the saint, which permeates through the sacred image, and to see with the heart as well as the mind.

Jonathan Lean was born in Fishguard in 1952. He undertook his ministerial training at Burgess Hall Lampeter in 1971. After completing his studies there in 1974 he was still too young to be ordained and was sent by Bishop Eric Roberts to the College of the Resurrection Mirfield. He was ordained to the diaconate in July 1975 and was priested the following year, serving his title at St Mary's Tenby. In 1981 he moved to be Vicar of Llanrhian, Llanhywel, and Llanrheithan (which now comprises part of the Rectorial Benefice of Dewisland). In 1988 Archbishop George Noakes invited him to be Vicar of St Martin's Haverfordwest and of St Ishmael's Lambston. In 2000 he was appointed Canon Residentiary of St Davids Cathedral and in 2001 Team Vicar of the newly created Rectorial Benefice of Dewisland, with responsibility for the Parish of St Davids. He became Dean and Precentor of St Davids Cathedral and the Rector of Dewisland in 2009.

Francis Northall was born in Birmingham and uses the traditional skills of a manufacturing jeweller, taught to him by a master craftsman over fifty years ago in The Jewellery Quarter of Birmingham. In the subsequent years he has honed those skills to produce high quality, hand-made pieces in all the noble metals. He has been commissioned to make a number of commemorative pieces and his greatest accolade was a commission to make a bracelet, as a present from her mother, for Lady Diana Spencer prior to her wedding. His work has been sold all over the United Kingdom and in Japan and America but mostly it has been retailed through some of the leading jewellers in London's West End. In 2003 he moved to Pembrokeshire and has his workshop in St Davids where he now lives. Recent commissions include a new mayoral chain for St Davids City Council and a pectoral cross for the Bishop of St Davids.

Jerry Sampson has been the Cathedral Archaeologist for St Davids Cathedral for 17 years and has worked on English and Welsh cathedrals since 1978, with projects at Wells, Exeter, Gloucester, Salisbury, Winchester, Rochester and Brecon, as well as vernacular buildings such as Montacute House, Wilton House and HM Tower of London. He began his career working under Dr Warwick Rodwell, the author of the standard textbook on church archaeology. He is a specialist buildings archaeologist and was responsible for the archaeological monitoring of the conservation and repair of Wells Cathedral west front 1980-87, designing recording systems which are now the 'industry standard'. Work at St Davids has included the detailed archaeological study of the standing fabric of the cloisters and Porth y Tŵr in order to inform their reconstruction and roofing, as well as a study of the presbytery roof and the west front during their repair and conservation.

Patrick Thomas was born in 1952 and studied English at St Catharine's College, Cambridge. He trained for the priesthood at the College of the Resurrection, Mirfield and served his title between 1979-1981 in the Rectorial Benefice of Aberystwyth. During this time he was also awarded a PhD from the University of Wales, Aberystwyth. In 1982 he was appointed Rector of the Llangeitho group of parishes and in 1984 he moved to be the incumbent of the Brechfa group of parishes. Since 2001 he has served as the Vicar of St David's and Christchurch, Carmarthen. He is an honorary member of the Gorsedd of Bards and has served on the Welsh Language Board. He was installed as a Canon of the Cathedral in 2000 and was appointed Canon Chancellor in 2009.

Harri Williams was born in Cardiff and spent a gap year in St Davids, working in the Cathedral. He studied modern history at Balliol College, Oxford. He trained for the priesthood at St Michael's College, Llandaff during which time he also studied theology at Cardiff University. He was ordained to the diaconate in 2010 and priested the following year and is currently the Assistant Curate of the Parish of Haverfordwest. Since September 2007 he has served as Secretary of the Friends of St Davids Cathedral.

Friend Wood was born in Watford, Hertfordshire and spent his early life in Australia and Pembrokeshire. He undertook his early training as an apprentice carpenter and joiner at Mac & Sons, Narberth and following this was employed at Pembrokeshire Crafts. Key projects during his time at Pembrokeshire Crafts included an altar table for The Parish Church of St Michael at the North Gate, Oxford and the creation of a shop, made entirely of limed oak, at the back of the nave of St Davids Cathedral. Throughout his career he has made all manner of different working models for the land, water and air. Highlights include the rebuilding of an *Isetta* bubble car found in Neyland in 1980; the ultra-aerodynamic, mahogany monocoque three-wheeled car *Tryane11* and most recently the wooden velomobile *WoodVM*.